1791

# THE OBSERVER

# Sayings of the Seventies

**Selected and compiled by**
Colin Cross

**David & Charles** Newton Abbot London
North Pomfret (Vt)

# To V. F.

**British Library Cataloguing in Publication Data**

'The Observer'
  Sayings of the seventies.
  1. Quotations, English
  I. Cross, Colin       II. Sayings of the seventies
  808.88'2              PN6081

ISBN 0 7153 7938 0

© The Observer Limited 1979

Set in Monotype Ehrhardt
and printed in Great Britain
by Western Printing Services Ltd, Bristol
for David & Charles (Publishers) Limited
Brunel House Newton Abbot Devon

Published in the United States of America
by David & Charles Inc
North Pomfret Vermont 05053 USA

# Introduction

The Seventies have been a decade during which—how to put it?—many things have changed. If the Sixties were 'swinging', then perhaps the Seventies are best characterised as 'surprising'. This compilation provides a more detailed look at the decade than later historians are likely to require, but will undoubtedly be fascinating to those who have actually lived through it.

The Sayings are collected, week by week, in the course of practical newspaper work. At *The Observer* we regard them as a sort of *hors d'oeuvre* before the main courses. Sometimes they are wise, witty, ridiculous or otherwise memorable. Sometimes they are totally ephemeral, of interest only in a particular week or even on a particular Sunday. The selection in this book has been made from among the more durable ones.

The rule is that the Sayings must always have occurred during the previous seven days, and this means we miss some beauties if we fail to get them straight off the bat. However, in the Seventies we have managed to catch 'Better a three-day week than a no-day week' (Edward Heath) and 'One man's pay increase is another man's price increase' (Harold Wilson). We also have a version of Mr Heath's 'unacceptable face of capitalism'.

There is no planned pattern to the weekly collection, and a retrospective look causes some surprises as well as confirming some expectations. Two women have kept cropping up: Princess Anne and Mrs Thatcher. Anwar Sadat is a regular among the men, as is Ian Smith. Idi Amin wins places without difficulty.

The feature has run in *The Observer* since 1917, and the book *Sayings of the Week*, published last year, covered the whole period 1917–78. The present volume follows the pattern of its predecessor, although of course there are essential differences in perspective in looking at one decade as opposed to sixty-one years. Some categories have vanished, notably Nationalisation and Psychologists. Patriotism is down to two entries, both of which the people of 1917 would probably have found surprising; Poverty has only one. Of course the test is not the intrinsic importance of a subject but the extent to which people have had quotable things to say about it. Some of the classifications are necessarily arbitrary. The new categories for the 1970s are Ambitions, Energy, Europe and Inflation.

Compiling the Sayings week by week is not always effortless. The sources are diverse, and some quotations have had

3

to be specially translated into English. Although they are chosen for a predominantly British readership, it is reckoned to be a British readership with an international outlook. By tradition, it is the Editor in person who has the final say as to what goes into the paper.

For this collection, personal titles and job descriptions of the Sayers are included only when they seem necessary for clarification, and are given as at the time when the words were uttered. Thus, for example, it is Lew Grade in the earlier part of the decade and later Lord Grade. The dates are those on which the quotations appeared in *The Observer*.

**Colin Cross, September 1979**

# Ambitions

I would like to be the head of an advertising agency.

*The Duchess of Windsor*, 18.1.1970

The truth, which I think we all have to recognise, is that people have always wanted to own their own homes, but now far more people have the money to do it than before.

*Julian Amery, speaking as Housing Minister on rising house prices*, 21.5.1972

I could end the Vietnam war and get our troops and prisoners home within 90 days.

*George McGovern*, 11.6.1972

I don't want to be just an ordinary player.

*George Best*, 10.12.1972

The Israelis must not be so ambitious as to think there is instant peace. It is an evolutionary process at the end of which you have normal relations.

*Anwar Sadat*, 24.3.1974

I want to earn an honest living.

*Ronald Biggs*, 12.5.1974

# The Arts

I think you can be contemporary without taking off your clothes.

*Robert Helpman*, 8.2.1970

Shakespeare is the sexiest great writer in the language.

*A L Rowse*, 25.4.1971

As a poet there is only one political duty, and that is to defend one's language against corruption. When it is corrupted people lose faith in what they hear and this leads to violence.

*W H Auden*, 31.10.1971

I like to be frightened when I see a film. Not to upset people would be an obscenity.

*Roman Polanski*, 30.1.1972

I don't think anyone is free—one creates one's own prison.

*Graham Sutherland*, 13.1.1974

Art is as important as council housing.

*Illtyd Harrington, Deputy Leader, GLC*, 25.5.1975

Poetry is an absolutely dead art—like taking up archery.

*Sacheverell Sitwell*, 29.8.1976

My Russian friends tell me it's not the Minister of Culture that you worry about. It's the culture of the Minister.

*Isaac Stern*, 18.12.1977

People have a sense of beauty and can appreciate nudity in films.

*Peking wall poster*, 7.1.1979

Broadcasting is nothing but a handmaid to the other arts.

*Sir William Haley*, 1.4.1979

# Bad Guesses

If I were a football manager, on present form I would be more worried about job security than I am as Prime Minister.

*Harold Wilson*, 5.4.1970

Writing about the Nixon Administration is about as exciting as covering the Prudential Life Assurance Company.

*Art Buchwald*, 19.7.1970

President Nixon's proposed visit to Peking has all the portents of taking its place with Munich and Yalta in a great trilogy of betrayal.

*Robert Morris, addressing the American Bar Association in London*, 25.7.1971

We have the happiest Africans in the world.

*Ian Smith*, 28.11.1971

For one union to take on the Government this year would
be damned suicide.

*Joe Gormley*, 18.2.1973

If there were a Labour Government tomorrow there would
be no question about it—a Labour Government would
have to produce a statutory incomes policy every bit as
stringent as the one imposed, and would be forced to resist
this and other strikes designed to break that policy.

*Dick Taverne, on a hospital strike*, 25.3.1973

Our problem at the moment is a problem of success.

*Edward Heath*, 18.11.1973

John Stonehouse must be a good man if he served in the
Labour Government.

*Sir Harold Walter, Mauritius Minister
for Health*, 20.4.1975

The last thing I ever wanted to do was to create a
national scandal.

*Norman Scott*, 6.8.1978

I should like very much to take a vacation.

*The Shah of Iran*, 7.1.1979

# Britain, the British ...

In close-up the British revolutionary Left seethes with
such repulsive, self-righteous dogmatists that it practically
drives one to enlist as a deck-hand on 'Morning Cloud'.

*Richard Neville*, 9.4.1972

Some have lost or spent all their money. Others have lost
their passports, their plane tickets and so on. Others have
lost their cars, some don't know where they are and others
are drunk.

*British Consulate spokesman in Barcelona, on Scottish
football fans*, 28.5.1972

It really is ludicrous that British waiters have to have Italian names because in some way it is thought to be more attractive to be an Italian waiter than a British waiter.

*William Rees-Davies, MP*, 13.8.1972

Our wages are lower, our holidays are shorter, our working hours are longer simply because we produce less per man employed. Unless we put this right, we risk becoming the peasants of the Western world.

*Michael Clapham, President, CBI*, 1.4.1973

The reason why nobody talks in England is because children are taught manners instead of conversation.

*Robert Morley*, 21.9.1975

The British public seems to abandon all sense of propriety and cleanliness when entering a public cafeteria and instantly assumes dirty habits.

*Egon Ronay*, 9.11.1975

The fashion nowadays is to say that Britain is in decline. You can read it in the Italian newspapers. But the Kaiser thought we were in decline and so did Hitler.

*Harold Macmillan*, 7.11.1976

The people of this country are not a community of boy scouts: they don't really want to rally round anyone.

*Lord Goodman*, 28.11.1976

We British must ski on.

*The Prince of Wales*, 4.2.1979

## ... and as others see us

The English have a rich oral folklore, of which the most famous items are the English folk ballads performed to the accompaniment of a harp or violin.

*New Soviet Encyclopaedia*, 29.3.1970

I always enjoy appearing before a British audience. Even
if they don't feel like laughing they nod their heads to
show they've understood.

*Bob Hope*, 8.11.1970

The British have three qualities: humour, tenacity and
realism. I sometimes think we are still at the humour stage.

*Georges Pompidou*, 24.1.1971

The eagerness of the British leaders to participate with
maximum personal visibility in bringing peace to Vietnam
was sometimes embarrassing to the United States.

*The Pentagon Papers*, 2.7.1972

English life, while very pleasant, is rather bland. I
expected kindness and gentility and I found it, but there is
such a thing as too much couth.

*S J Perelman*, 24.9.1972

You have a Welfare State. But I have walked your streets
at night and gone into your homes and found people dying
unloved. Here you have a different kind of poverty. A
poverty of spirit, of loneliness and being unwanted. And
that is the worst disease in the world: not tuberculosis or
leprosy.

*Mother Teresa of Calcutta*, 29.4.1973

Britain has traits of the impoverished aristocrat and Italy
of the historically poor.

*Ralf Dahrendorf*, 17.10.1976

## Broadcasting

A television service which bore no relation to the viewers'
own experience of the world would quickly lose their
respect and ultimately their allegiance.

*David Attenborough*, 2.4.1972

Children watch too much television not only because
indolent parents allow them to, but because the standard
of most programmes is pitched at their level.

*Richard Ingrams*, 18.9.1977

Three things are specifically excluded from our television—political propaganda against the socialist system, sadism and pornography.

*Richard Nagy, Director-General, Hungarian Television,*
*25.6.1978*

The Pope's got great charisma. I'd like to sign him up.

*Lord Grade, 21.1.1979*

# The Civil Service

We've produced figures showing that if you sack a civil servant he will cost the community more by being sacked than his present wages.

*Ken Thomas, Civil and Public Services*
*Association, 16.5.1976*

You can cut any public expenditure except the Civil Service; those lads have spent a hundred years learning to look after themselves.

*Richard Marsh, 19.9.1976*

I do not think any Minister should shelter behind his civil servants.

*Harold Wilson, 6.3.1977*

Our members will do precisely what is in their contracts without a smile.

*Frank Huff, regional officer, National Union of Public*
*Employees, 28.1.1979*

# Communism

Our Vatican is neither in Moscow nor in Peking, Havana or Belgrade. It is in Chile.

*Salvador Allende, 1.11.1970*

The *Pravda* article appears to pay too little attention to the different conditions for the advance of socialism which exist in different countries, and to deal with tactics applicable in Russia at the time at which Lenin wrote as if they were universally applicable today.

*George Matthews, head of the Communist Party's press and publicity department*, 17.8.1975

The world Communist movement is no longer a Church, and Moscow is no longer Rome.

*Santiago Carrillo, Spanish Communist leader*, 3.7.1977

Chairman Mao was a man not a god. The time has come to give him his real place.

*Peking wall poster*, 26.11.1978

For us in Russia Communism is a dead dog, while for many people in the West it is still a living lion.

*Alexander Solzhenitsyn*, 18.2.1979

# Definitions

English is no longer the language of England alone. It is above all and in the eyes of the world the language of America.

*Georges Pompidou*, 23.5.1971

I did not know I was a radical or a nationalist. I thought I was a person.

*Abel Muzorewa*, 13.2.1972

A study of history shows that civilisations that abandon the quest for knowledge are doomed to disintegration.

*Sir Bernard Lovell*, 14.5.1972

Cattle-rustling is probably the major growth industry in Scotland.

*William Hamilton, MP*, 11.3.1973

Pipe-smokers are patient, reasonable men, prepared to hear their victims' point of view.

*Hugh Cudlipp*, 25.11.1973

If you buy land on which is a slagheap 120 feet high and it costs £100,000 to remove it, that is not speculation but land reclamation.

*Harold Wilson*, 7.4.1974

The value of the pound is what the market says it is.

*Milton Friedman*, 3.10.1976

A poet and a revolutionary—that is what I have been all these years and that is how I shall remain until the last breath is gone from my body.

*Zulfikar Ali Bhutto*, 11.2.1979

There is but one thing more dangerous than sin—the murder of a man's sense of sin.

*Pope John Paul II*, 8.4.1979

# Economics

Better a three-day week than a no-day week.

*Edward Heath*, 28.7.1974

Never in the history of human credit has so much been owed.

*Margaret Thatcher*, 12.10.1975

I have always thought it was the first task of an economist to provide himself with a certain minimum of money. The fact I was able to do that without too much mental strain has never bothered me.

*John Kenneth Galbraith*, 2.11.1975

I will consider selling off the Crown Jewels—but I am not absolutely certain that they are the property of Her Majesty's Government.

*Denis Healey*, 19.12.1976

Paying people more just because they get so little is a recipe for disaster.

*Frank Chapple, General Secretary, Electrical, Electronic, Telecommunications and Plumbing Union*, 25.2.1979

The Archangel Gabriel in charge of all the computers in the world could not produce comparable rates of pay throughout the public sector.

*Jo Grimond*, 18.3.1979

# Education

No normal parent will ever accept the judgement of a test, however apparently fair, that their child of only 11 is a failure.

*Edward Short, Secretary of State for Education*, 15.2.1970

The lowest paid private entering the army on 1 April this year will get £14 7s a week—a pound more than my own daughter is getting as a teacher.

*Denis Healey*, 1.3.1970

Co-education is unutterably unimportant.

*Ruth Cohen, Principal, Newnham College, Cambridge*, 3.10.1971

Today students are no longer legal infants. Parliament has made them adults.

*Lord Annan*, 5.11.1972

I would close down any school where most of the children are not reading by the age of seven.

*Rhodes Boyson*, 23.2.1975

No sensible person suggests that students should not learn about Marxism, any more than that a medical course should omit venereal disease.

*Professor C K Grant, Durham University*, 22.11.1977

The biggest weakness of comprehensive schools is that they are not comprehensive schools.

*Max Morris, executive member, National Union of Teachers*, 8.1.1978

Comprehensive schools demonstrate that we are all members of one family, of one society.

*Shirley Williams*, 21.1.1979

13

Eton, and indeed the independent sector of secondary education as a whole, has in the national interest a positive obligation to survive.

*Lord Charteris, Provost of Eton,* 18.3.1979

Despite the pontifications of professors, the bletherings of sociologists and the double-talk of Ministers, every teacher and parent knows that small classes are needed if the schools are to do their best.

*Max Morris,* 22.4.1979


# Energy

The era of low-cost energy is almost dead. Popeye has run out of cheap spinach.

*Peter Peterson, US Commerce Secretary,* 19.11.1972

If sunbeams were weapons of war we would have had solar energy long ago.

*Sir George Porter, Director, British Association,* 26.8.1973

Sunday is the one time of the week that we ought to use as much gasoline as possible: if our country ever needed the Lord it is now.

*Billy Graham,* 25.11.1973

There is no way to win on energy legislation.

*Jimmy Carter,* 12.11.1978

Our energy policy is to ring as many alarm bells as we can.

*Roy Jenkins, President, EEC Commission,* 4.3.1979

We are in a situation that is not a situation we have ever been in before.

*Dudley Thomson, US Nuclear Regulatory Commission,* 8.4.1979

# Equality

I am not the product of privilege. I am the product of opportunity.

*Edward Heath*, 17.2.1974

Half the country is middle class: the other half is trying to be.

*Alan Ayckbourn*, 20.3.1977

Neither Marxism nor liberalism can solve our central problem: the problem of order, or as I put it, fraternity.

*Professor A H Halsey*, 19.2.1978

The language down the pit is no worse than in a ladies' shoe shop.

*Tom Lindop, member of Newcastle-under-Lyme Industrial Tribunal*, 14.1.1979

If I cannot afford to buy food, why should anyone else have it?

*Bill Astbury, Chairman, Greater Manchester Lorry Drivers' Strike Committee*, 21.1.1979

Everyone has a right to work and everyone has the right to pass a picket line.

*James Callaghan*, 28.1.1979

# Europe

Most of our Continental neighbours have got sharper minds than ours.

*Enoch Powell*, 8.3.1970

I have read articles and speeches which make you think that every British worker is living on steak and strawberries and his wretched Continental brothers on scrag and stew.

*Lord George-Brown*, 11.7.1971

I have a soft spot even for the inefficient farmers in Provence and the Dordogne. I like their *coq au vin*.

*Michael Foot*, 1.8.1971

We must recapture our European voice, the voice all of us instinctively realise, a voice of reason, of humanity, of moderation, which can be heard throughout the world.

*Edward Heath*, 22.10.1972

When Britain is about to enter the EEC it is somewhat tactless to print on the back of the £5 note a picture of British gunners blowing the French army to blazes and accompanying it with a large portrait of the Duke of Wellington.

*Lord Leatherland*, 12.11.1972

If the European Community goes on doing nothing, always following the slowest ship in the convoy, then one day the slowest ship will stop.

*Willy Brandt*, 24.11.1974

I do not see the EEC as a great love affair. It is more like nine middle-aged couples with failing marriages meeting at a Brussels hotel for a group grope.

*Kenneth Tynan*, 11.5.1975

It is appropriate that the Referendum took place on the feast of St Boniface, one of the first Englishmen to go into Europe and stay there.

*Rev C B Cunningham*, 15.6.1975

If the European Community collapses, then Germany could survive, but I don't know who else could.

*Helmut Schmidt*, 7.12.1975

I've never been one to say that Britain was joining a happy band of brothers.

*James Callaghan, on the EEC*, 5.12.1976

I'd be much more worried about the European Economic Community if nobody wanted to join us.

*Roy Jenkins*, 17.4.1977

# Fashion

Hot pants are the limit. People complain you are not with it, but certain things I will not do.

*Princess Anne, 11.4.1971*

God is no longer fashionable. Our vision of reality is dazzled by the splendour and interest of science. There is no longer the calmness of spirit enabling us to confront our experience with more stable and higher principles.

*Pope Paul VI, 27.5.1973*

Generally speaking, most people are now in favour of children. This was not so in the 18th century.

*Lord Hale, 16.12.1973*

The moustache will not be longer than the mouth and it will not be grown below the top lip. I don't want to see my lads looking like a lot of cissies.

*Regimental Sergeant-Major Beattie of the Black Watch, 18.8.1974*

# Food and Drink

We are wealthy and wasteful but this can't go on. If we don't eat dog biscuits, we could end up eating our dog instead.

*Magnus Pyke, 12.1.1975*

When MPs visit you, please remember at least to offer to feed them.

*Cyril Smith, 4.5.1975*

Anyone who says you can bargain around the world for cheap food is talking tosh.

*Fred Peart, 1.6.1975*

Food, or to be more precise, lack of it, may well surpass all other crises and troubles that beset us.

*Lord Rothschild, 21.11.1976*

Who wouldn't eat caviare if it was offered?

*Reginald Maudling, 2.10.1977*

Maybe it picks you up a little bit, but it sure lets you down in a hurry.

*Betty Ford, on alcohol,* 11.2.1979

# Freedom and Liberty

Everyone seemed to want an election.

*Harold Wilson,* 24.5.1970

If you want democracy, a little bit of inefficiency must be accepted.

*Hugh Cubitt, Leader, Westminster City Council,* 13.8.1972

This is a free country and anybody is entitled to ask for anything.

*Len Murray,* 20.1.1974

If dictatorship is the concentration of power, freedom consists in its diffusion.

*Lord Hailsham,* 1.2.1976

The price of championing human rights is a little inconsistency from time to time.

*David Owen,* 3.4.1977

No word in the vocabulary has been so debased and abused as democracy.

*Lord Shawcross,* 24.4.1977

To say a thing is natural is to condone it, never to praise it.

*Quentin Crisp,* 5.2.1978

We do not believe that bread and liberty are incompatible.

*Morarji Desai,* 1.6.1978

If someone is confronting our essential liberties, if someone is inflicting injury and harm—by God, I'll confront them.

*Margaret Thatcher,* 4.2.1979

If they ban smoking, it won't be long before some nut wants to ban drinking with darts.

*Olly Croft, Secretary, British Darts Organisation,* 18.2.1979

# Futurology

I see the time coming when people will regard it as a duty to use contraceptives rather than a duty not to.

> *Hugh Montefiore, Bishop-designate of*
> *Kingston-upon-Thames, 25.1.1970*

One in every six girls and one in every nine boys now at school must expect to spend some period of their lives as inmates of mental hospitals.

> *David Ennals, 13.6.1971*

In developing our industrial strategy for the period ahead, we have the benefit of much experience. Almost everything has been tried at least once.

> *Tony Benn, 17.3.1974*

There are going to be no dramatic changes in Rhodesia.

> *Ian Smith, 5.1.1975*

My idea of a Labour Government is one which fulfils its election pledges to build a new Jerusalem, which is not a corny ideal.

> *Eric Heffer, 13.7.1975*

All of us are standing on the brink of a great historical cataclysm, a flood that swallows up civilisation and changes whole epochs.

> *Alexander Solzhenitsyn, 28.3.1976*

By the end of 1991 it is not unreasonable to suppose that motoring will become an occupation indulged in by the super-rich, just as it was in the early 1920s.

> *Lord Tanlaw, 29.5.1977*

So consider, take heed of what I say
This day you rule, tomorrow I hold sway.

> *Final lines of a sonnet by the computer at Nene College,*
> *Northampton, 5.3.1978*

If paternity leave was granted it would result in a direct incitement to a population explosion.

> *Ian Gow, MP, 4.2.1979*

I will be the one who will choose the Government with the
support of the people.

*Ayatollah Khomeini*, 4.2.1979

When changes occur in the Soviet regime, the whole orbit
of life on earth will change.

*Alexander Solzhenitsyn*, 25.2.1979

# Homespun Philosophy

Making money ain't nothing exciting to me. You might be
able to buy a little better booze than the wino on the
corner. But you get sick just like the next cat and when you
die you're just as graveyard dead.

*Louis Armstrong*, 5.7.1970

History teaches us that men and nations behave wisely once
they have exhausted all other alternatives.

*Abba Eban, Israeli Foreign Minister*, 20.12.1970

What keeps me going is curiosity. I am longing to discover
things about the past as well as look into the future and I
care about what happens. That is what does it: curiosity
and caring.

*Arnold Toynbee, at 82*, 12.3.1972

To be successful, keep looking tanned, live in an elegant
building (even if you're in the cellar), be seen in smart
restaurants (even if you nurse one drink) and if you borrow,
borrow big.

*Aristotle Onassis*, 20.8.1972

Nothing is surely a waste of time when one enjoys the day.

*Arthur Koestler*, 8.10.1972

There are hazards in anything one does, but there are
greater hazards in doing nothing.

*Shirley Williams*, 16.6.1974

The belief in progress, the belief that man can manage his destiny is the most appalling death wish that ever afflicted humanity.

*Malcolm Muggeridge*, 4.8.1974

Running a country is like playing the organ. You have to use all the stops—pull out one, pull back the other. It's not like playing the penny whistle.

*Harold Macmillan*, 10.11.1974

What one generation sees as a luxury, the next sees as a necessity.

*Anthony Crosland*, 22.6.1975

The simple belief in automatic material progress by means of scientific discovery and application is a tragic myth of our age.

*Sir Bernard Lovell*, 31.8.1975

People always seem to forget that a hawk is always in the sky ready to swoop on the chickens.

*Jomo Kenyatta*, 19.10.1975

When you're hot, anything can happen.

*Jimmy Connors*, 27.6.1976

There is no such thing as the pursuit of happiness, but there is the discovery of joy.

*Joyce Grenfell*, 12.9.1976

We live in a world of rapid change and if we are to survive in such a world we must be prepared to adjust ourselves to change.

*Ian Smith*, 26.9.1976

A little uncertainty is good for everyone.

*Henry Kissinger*, 12.12.1976

The Community is not a betting shop or a lottery stall into which one takes one's stakes and hopes to come away with more than one went in.

*Roy Jenkins*, 16.1.1977

You can never reach the promised land. You can march
towards it.

*James Callaghan*, 23.7.78

There's nothing more precious in this world than the
feeling of being wanted.

*Diana Dors*, 24.9.1978

Heaven on earth is not tomorrow.

*James Callaghan*, 18.2.1979

# Industry and Work

During the clergy conference a skeleton staff will be
maintained for cemetery duty.

*Diocesan leaflet*, 16.7.1972

For colour vision, ability to distinguish between red and
black is the only requirement.

*Note to applicants for jobs in a bank*, 4.2.1973

I have told the country before that capitalism has its
unacceptable face. If you want to see the acceptable face of
capitalism, go out to an oil rig in the North Sea.

*Edward Heath*, 24.2.1974

I cannot say in all truth that I do look on capitalism
and business with the same joy as in 1960.

*Jim Slater*, 2.6.1974

The fact that a business is large, efficient and profitable
does not mean that it takes advantage of the public.

*Charles Clore*, 30.6.1974

The efficiency of an enterprise is much more important
than the question of who owns the shares.

*Reg Prentice*, 11.8.1974

The success of our pay policy has been accompanied by a
dramatic improvement in our industrial relations.

*Denis Healey*, 6.2.1977

Working class people spend most of their time and money drinking and smoking.

*A L Rowse*, 17.4.1977

We must destroy the work ethic. No longer must a person's social position be judged by his paid occupation.

*Clive Jenkins*, 17.9.1978

I am sick and tired of pushing top managers to work long hours and weekends when I know they are not getting a fair deal themselves.

*Michael Edwardes, Chairman, British Leyland*, 21.1.1979

To compare people who go on strike with terrorists is nonsense, and dangerous nonsense.

*Len Murray*, 25.2.1979

# Inflation

One man's pay increase is another man's price increase.

*Harold Wilson*, 11.1.1970

If the present 8 per cent inflation rate were to be followed by 10 per cent there would be a danger of cantering inflation turning into galloping.

*Roy Jenkins*, 31.1.1971

The growth of inflation all over the world in the last 18 months is something which can bring much of the Western world, as we know it, to an end.

*Henry d'Avigdor-Goldsmid, MP*, 27.7.1973

A wages explosion at this time could blow up a lot more than the Retail Prices Index.

*Len Murray*, 7.7.1974

We have a love–hate relationship with inflation. We hate inflation but we love everything that causes it.

*William Simon, US Treasury Secretary*, 30.3.1975

Why do they call it a 'floating pound' when all it does is sink?

*Letter to The Times*, 29.6.1975

The dangers of inflation can scarcely be exaggerated, yet there are some in our ranks who would have us ignore the phenomenon as some sort of capitalistic trick.

*Jack Jones, 14.12.1975*

More Governments, including left-wing Governments, have been thrown out of power through a failure to deal with inflation than through any other single cause.

*Michael Foot, 18.4.1976*

Half a million pounds doesn't go far nowadays.

*Lord Butler of Saffron Walden, 21.5.1978*

# Ireland

There is not a single injustice in Northern Ireland that is worth the loss of a single British soldier, or a single Irish citizen either.

*James Callaghan, 12.4.1970*

Without divine intervention I would not have been able to defeat the Unionist Party machine.

*Ian Paisley, 26.4.1970*

I want to see peace, prosperity and happiness in my country, and I think the way we are going about achieving it is the best way.

*Joe Cahill, leader of the Belfast Provisional IRA,*
*12.9.1971*

I'll never go out with a soldier again. If you live in the Bogside you must live by the rules.

*Londonderry girl after being tarred and feathered,*
*14.11.1971*

My only regret is that I didn't seize Mr Maudling by the throat.

*Bernadette Devlin, 6.2.1972*

A large part of the sickness of Ulster stems from people who want to pick and choose which laws they will respect and which ignore: and from those who assert their rights but recognise no obligations.

*Brian Faulkner, Northern Ireland politician, 2.4.1972*

It will be my constant desire [in Ireland] to prove to people that I say what I mean and I really can be believed. At the moment I find it very difficult to achieve these simple tasks.

*William Whitelaw, 7.5.1972*

You lying BBC: you're photographing things that aren't happening.

*Woman in Belfast, attacking a BBC cameraman, 3.9.1972*

Others may think what they like, but we know our bombs blasted the Northern Ireland Parliament out of existence.

*Sean MacStiofain, Chief of Staff, Provisional IRA, 24.9.1972*

To paper over cracks can cause them to become chasms.

*Jack Lynch, Prime Minister of Ireland, 15.1.1978*

# Israel

I declare to the whole world that we agree to live with you in a permanent and just peace.

*Anwar Sadat, to the Israeli Knesset, 27.11.1977*

I think we have achieved peace, thanks to Jimmy.

*Anwar Sadat, 18.3.1979*

Mark my words, united Jerusalem is the eternal capital of Israel.

*Menachem Begin, 25.3.1979*

From Indonesia to Iran and from Saudi Arabia to Morocco there are hundreds of millions of Muslims with a vital stake in our holy city of Jerusalem.

*Crown Prince Fahd of Saudi Arabia, 25.3.1979*

We are a quasi-biblical generation and I want to write a book about it.

*Menachem Begin*, 1.4.1979

Whoever believes that the Jewish State in 1980 can control 1,250,000 reluctant Arabs by machine-gun and by imposing curfews is leading Israel to catastrophe.

*Moshe Dayan*, 22.4.1979

## Law and Lawyers

Civility is to the courtroom what antisepsis is to a hospital.

*Warren E Burger, US Chief Justice*, 30.5.1971

A man who is nothing but a lawyer is not much of a lawyer.

*Lord Goodman*, 9.1.1972

If a man can afford to pay for justice he will secure it.
A man who cannot afford to pay will rarely secure it.

*Gerald Nabarro*, 29.10.1972

I am old-fashioned enough to dislike sending women to prison.

*Judge Edward Clarke, QC*, 14.4.1974

To every subject in this land, no matter how powerful, I would use Thomas Fuller's words 300 years ago: 'Be you ever so high, the law is above you.'

*Lord Denning*, 30.1.1977

I would rather search for justice than search for certainty.

*Lord Denning*, 28.1.1979

Anyone who says people don't get away with murder is crazy.

*Michael Genelin, Los Angeles County Prosecutor*, 25.2.1979

There is a limit to what a man is entitled to say in temper or at any time.

*Mrs Justice Heilbron*, 4.3.1979

If only I was a dictator I'd pass a law preventing any pregnant girl from getting married. She'd have to wait a year until after the child was born.

*Sir George Baker, President, Family Division of the High Court,* 11.3.1979

Adultery remains a crime in New York State.

*Joseph Gagliardi, State Supreme Court Justice,* 22.4.1979

# Life and Living

To win your battle in this society, you've got to have your cave. Then food. Then some kind of mate. After that, everything's a luxury.

*Rod Steiger,* 25.1.1970

Saddest movie I've ever seen—I cried all the way through. It's sad when you're 82.

*Groucho Marx, on 'Last Tango in Paris',* 15.4.1973

You couldn't live 82 years in the world without being disillusioned.

*Dame Rebecca West,* 7.9.1975

If one starts from the premise that life is boring, then one should equip the child for it in the schools.

*Terence Ellis, headmaster of William Tyndale School, Islington,* 11.1.1976

People who are anti-dog are anti-sex.

*Jilly Cooper,* 24.4.1977

Ideally I'd like to spend two evenings a week talking to Proust and another conversing to the Holy Ghost.

*Edna O'Brien,* 21.8.1977

People are always sending me pictures of their aspidistras.

*Gracie Fields,* 10.9.1978

I have never filled in a pools coupon, so I have never been a winner. But I am going to have a shot from now on.

*Margaret Thatcher*, 25.3.1979

# Love and Marriage

I do not see why any wife should be expected to go back to a husband who said he did not love her.

*Mr Justice Park*, 23.5.1971

This diamond has so many carats, it's almost a turnip.

*Richard Burton, on his present to Elizabeth Taylor*, 5.3.1972

With these few words I want to assure you that I love you and if you had been a woman I would have considered marrying you, although your head is full of grey hairs, but as you are a man that possibility doesn't arise.

*Idi Amin, in a letter to President Nyerere of Tanzania*, 27.8.1972

I think everybody really will concede that on this, of all days, I should begin my speech with the words 'My husband and I'.

*The Queen, on her 25th wedding anniversary*, 26.11.1972

In these days of Women's Lib there is no reason why a wife, whose marriage has not lasted and who has no child, should have a bread ticket for life.

*Sir George Baker, President, giving judgement in the Family Division of the High Court*, 4.3.1973

I don't know of any young man, black or white, who doesn't have a girl friend besides his wife. Some have four sneaking around.

*Muhammad Ali*, 28.9.1975

If you are human you love and doubt. The only thing there shouldn't be any doubt about is your wife. If there is, it's finished.

*Marc Chagall*, 10.7.1977

Amorance, or being in love, is a cognitive affective state characterised by intrusive and obsessive fantasising concerning reciprocity of amorant feelings by the object of the amorance.

*American delegate to the Conference of Love and Attraction,*
11.9.1977

There's no substitute for moonlight and kissing.

*Barbara Cartland*, 11.9.1977

Marriage is rather a silly habit.
*John Osborne*, 1.6.1978

I long for a way out to accommodate second marriages.

*Donald Coggan, Archbishop of Canterbury*, 16.7.1978

There's simply no other way for a man to feel his manliness, his kingliness if you will, than to be loved by a beautiful woman.
*Tony Curtis*, 21.1.1979

I love men like some people like good food or wine.

*Germaine Greer*, 18.2.1979

There is a codeword which opens safes—it is LOVE.

*Notice in West German Government offices*, 18.3.1979

I wrote out a little list of questions for Pierre to put to the Pope about our marriage problems.

*Margaret Trudeau*, 8.4.1979

One wife at a time is enough for most people.

*Mr Justice Smith*, 13.5.1979

# Medicine

If one were to use cannabis as simply a new drug which might be introduced to medicine, the evidence we already have of health hazards would rule it out.

*William Paton, Professor of Pharmacology, Oxford,*
21.3.1971

There is no human activity, eating, drinking, sleeping or
sex, which some doctors somewhere won't discover leads
directly to cardiac arrest.

*John Mortimer, QC, 20.8.1978*

To anyone who says our health service is the best in the
world, I say: 'Fiddlesticks!'

*Reginald Murley, President, Royal College of Surgeons,
28.1.1979*

Prostitutes have a great therapeutic value.

*Maureen Colquhoun, 11.3.1979*

# Men

Men are people, just like women.

*Fenella Fielding, 20.6.1971*

He loves antiques and I think that's why he fell for me.

*Hermione Gingold, 74, announcing her engagement to an
antique dealer, 4.7.1971*

Men must be the leaders. That's why they have glorious
plumage, like peacocks, and the little grey females must go
where they direct.

*The Duchess of Bedford, 8.12.1974*

We have nothing against man cricketers. Some of them
are quite nice people, even though they don't win as often
as we do.

*Rachel Hayhoe-Flint, captain of the England women's
cricket team, 21.12.1975*

A man who steals his neighbour's wife may still be more
anti-social than one who steals his watch.

*Lord Longford, 18.1.1976*

Never despise what it says in the women's magazines: it
may not be subtle but neither are men.

*Zsa Zsa Gabor, 11.4.1976*

Few bosses would tell a male clerk to brew up a pot of tea.

*John Forrester, Amalgamated Union of Engineering Workers,*
*23.5.1976*

Just as most women like male gynaecologists, I think most men like lady vasectomists. One of my most masculine patients said: 'It's sort of natural taking off your trousers in front of a woman.'

*Dr Caroline Deys, 11.7.1976*

Women would not be prostitutes if it were not for men.

*Baroness Vickers, 3.7.1977*

I loved Kirk so much I would have skiied down Mount Everest in the nude with a carnation up my nose.

*Joyce McKinney, in the Mormon missionary case,*
*11.12.1977*

So many men find it hard to react if a girl says to them at a party: 'What's your telephone number? I'll call you tomorrow.'

*Jackie Collins, 16.4.1978*

Male chauvinist is a simple, idiotic way of describing him.

*Kate Millett, on Ayatollah Khomeini, 18.3.1979*

The Government is making the dangerous assumption that the head of a household is always a man.

*Gemma Hussey, Irish Senator, 25.3.1979*

Once you pass through the door of Number 10 Downing Street, you are in a world that is entirely male-orientated.

*Lady Falkender, 15.4.1979*

A man ought not to give up work and turn himself into a mother figure.

*Mr Justice Payne, 27.5.1979*

# Miaow!

I am sure Mr Heath thinks he is honest. But I wish he didn't have to have his friends say it so often.

*Roy Jenkins, 31.5.1970*

Sartre's thirst for martyrdom isn't enough to put someone so incurably inoffensive in prison.

*François Mauriac*, 17.6.1973

The House will note that this Government which has proclaimed more states of emergency than any other, has now appropriately completed its record by being the only one in history to leave the nation in a state of emergency and without a Parliament.

*Roy Jenkins*, 10.2.1974

If I rescued a child from drowning, the Press would no doubt headline the story 'Benn grabs child'.

*Tony Benn*, 2.3.1975

Mrs Castle is like an inverted version of Lord Kitchener.

*Jeremy Thorpe*, 8.6.1975

Gaddafi is the lunatic of Libya—a dwarf who thought he was a giant.

*Anwar Sadat*, 25.7.1976

Sadat and Begin remind me of the musical 'Annie Get Your Gun'—anything you can do I can do better.

*Yitzhak Rabin, Israeli politician*, 12.3.1978

Karpov beat me unfairly. It was the struggle of the State against the individual.

*Anatov Korchnoi*, 22.10.1978

I am a great friend of Israel. Any country that can stand Milton Friedman as an adviser has nothing to fear from a few million Arabs.

*John Kenneth Galbraith*, 4.2.1979

# Milestones

France is a widow.

*President Pompidou, on the death of Charles de Gaulle*,
15.11.1970

The era of cheap food is over.

> *Lord Watkinson, Chairman, Cadbury Schweppes,*
> *31.12.1972*

It is the unpleasant or unacceptable face of capitalism.

> *Edward Heath, on Lonrho, 20.5.1973*

We cannot undo what has been done. The sum of the suffering and the horror cannot be removed from the consciousness of our people.

> *Chancellor Willy Brandt, on his arrival in Israel,*
> *10.6.1973*

I do not expect to be impeached.

> *Richard Nixon, 3.3.1974*

We have learnt that a Government which deceives its supporters and treats its opponents as enemies must never, never be tolerated.

> *Gerald Ford, 20.10.1974*

I never thought a man like Dr Kissinger would deliver our people to such a disastrous fate.

> *Ex-President Thieu of South Vietnam, 27.4.1975*

I am proud of democracy in the country and do not want to do anything against it.

> *Indira Gandhi, 6.7.1975*

What do you mean by Watergate—the building?

> *One of Richard Nixon's lawyers, 24.8.1975*

I ask pardon from all, as with all my heart I forgive those who declared themselves my enemies—not that I considered them such.

> *Francisco Franco's last message to the Spanish people,*
> *23.11.1975*

The crunch, so long awaited, so often discussed, is now upon us.

> *Edward Heath, 10.10.1976*

Democracy has begun.

*King Juan Carlos of Spain*, 24.7.1977

We have fulfilled the commitment we gave to the Scottish
people.

*James Callaghan*, 11.3.1979

I have got to admit that things haven't gone quite the way
I wanted.

*Ian Smith*, 3.6.1979

## Modesty

People call me the Enoch Powell of sex.

*Lord Longford*, 29.8.1971

I'm not a capitalist.

*'Tiny' Rowland*, 3.6.1973

Mr Kanso Yoshida, cousin of the Emperor Hirohito of
Japan, has died in Liverpool aged 78. Since he came to
Liverpool in 1912, Mr Yoshida has been known as Paddy
Murphy.

*Liverpool Free Press*, 29.7.1973

I rise to present my Budget in a mood of humility and
trepidation—a mood which I fear may not have
characterised all my contributions to our debates in the
past.

*Denis Healey*, 31.3.1974

I owe nothing to Women's Lib.

*Margaret Thatcher*, 1.12.1974

I fear no one but God.

*Idi Amin*, 27.2.1977

I let down my friends. I let down my country. I let down
our system of government.

*Richard Nixon*, 8.5.1977

I have no intention—no present intention—of standing for Parliament.

*Harold Macmillan, 18.2.1979*

Naturists would pollute the beach.

*Councillor Lillian Cade of Bournemouth, 25.2.1979*

I call myself a lucky barber.

*Vidal Sassoon, 18.3.1979*


# Money

Nobody will persuade me there is no money about when I see so much spent on gambling, foreign travel, glossy magazines and plastic gnomes in every front garden.

*Sir Frederick Seebohm, Chairman, Barclays Bank, 14.2.1971*

There is no cure for the lack of a pay check but another pay check.

*Joseph Curry, New York State Employment Service, 4.4.1971*

That's not too bad is it. At least not for him. It would be a life's savings for me.

*Albert Steward, Lord Lambton's butler, on a £300 fine imposed on Lord Lambton for possessing drugs, 17.6.1973*

The requirements of a successful Governor of the Bank of England are the tact and skill of an ambassador and the guile of a Romanian horse thief.

*Harold Lever, 27.1.1974*

Money is not so important as a pat on the head.

*Lord Snow, 18.12.1977*

There is no one, but no one, in this House who would do the job these people are doing for a take-home pay of about £40 a week.

*Denis Skinner, MP, on gravediggers, 4.2.1979*

## Music and Musicians

Beethoven is about trying to get on with your wife. It is a reconciliation of opposites.

*Colin Davis*, 16.8.1970

Most people are acoustically deaf and don't even notice the acoustic pollution of the world.

*Karlheinz Stockhausen*, 19.9.1971

I do believe that young composers should have to struggle a certain amount, but they shouldn't have to look around for the price of a bit of bread.

*Dmitri Shostakovich*, 23.7.1972

I know I have a reputation for bad tempers, but I am always having good tempers.

*Maria Callas*, 17.12.1972

I have made my contribution to society. I have no plans to work again.

*John Lennon*, 30.10.1977

When the tape is good and the music flows the elation is like making love.

*Art Garfunkel*, 22.4.1979

You cannot sing 'La Traviata' in a mini-skirt.

*Tito Gobbi*, 13.5.1979

## On the Record

I do not want to be the Pétain of Egypt.

*Gamal Abdel Nasser*, 22.2.1970

I have a horror of the word 'tasteful'.

*Kenneth Tynan*, 9.8.1970

This Bill [Industrial Relations] will not be allowed to go through Parliament on its stockinged feet.

*Victor Feather*, 17.1.1971

I did it because I'm the Devil and the Devil always has a bald head.

> *Charles Manson, appearing in court with a shaved head,*
> 7.3.1971

I am a lone monk walking the world with a leaky umbrella.

> *Mao Tse Tung, 9.5.1971*

Certain things happened during the Second World War for which I feel personally sorry.

> *Emperor Hirohito of Japan, 21.11.1971*

The driver shall cause his vehicle to enter the Tunnel via the entrance and, after proceeding through the Tunnel, to leave via an exit.

> *Draft regulation for Kingsway Tunnel, Liverpool,*
> 12.12.1971

I believe in private property.

> *Svetlana Alliluyeva, daughter of Josef Stalin,*
> 27.2.1972

With the wolves swooping down, the shepherd does not desert his flock.

> *Archbishop Makarios, 18.6.1972*

Nobody will make me become an English citizen again. The only possible reason would be for tax reasons.

> *W H Auden, 25.6.1972*

Some of us do not accept the Establishment myth that bad laws must be obeyed.

> *Tom Driberg, 30.7.1972*

If the criminal wants to commit suicide then he should be allowed to do so. Something should be left in the cell. Perhaps a razor blade.

> *Jonathan Guiness, Conservative candidate in the Lincoln*
> *by-election, 25.2.1973*

I would have been deeply offended if they had left me off that list.

> *John Kenneth Galbraith, on the White House blacklist,*
> 1.7.1973

I refuse to lead a nation of drunkards. I would sooner die.

*Kenneth Kaunda*, 11.11.1973

My own view is that taping of conversations for historical purposes was a bad decision.

*Richard Nixon*, 19.5.1974

I am a bit of a showman—and I don't mind admitting it.

*Jeremy Thorpe*, 8.9.1974

If the fence is strong enough, I'll sit on it.

*Cyril Smith*, 15.9.1974

I have been a fighter all my life.

*Edward Heath*, 2.2.1975

I am convinced that UFOs exist, because I have seen one.

*Jimmy Carter*, 6.6.1976

I can tell the difference between refuse from a council house and refuse from a private estate. Private people leave nice dustbins. Council estate dustbins are full to overflowing and they smell.

*Brian Hammond, Refuse Collector of the Year*, 6.6.1976

I myself consider I am the most powerful figure in the world.

*Idi Amin*, 15.8.1976

We don't hold many functions where the presence of a beauty queen is required.

*Councillor John Stanley, Mayor of Barnsley*, 12.3.1978

I have lived so long with realities that I am shock-proof.

*John Vorster*, 7.5.1978

We may be a hobbled tiger but we don't intend to become a lame duck.

*Sir Terence Beckett, Chairman, British Ford*, 3.12.1978

I'm not having my picture taken with that ruddy bear.

*Christopher Robin Milne*, 20.5.1979

I am glad that justice was done.

*Jeremy Thorpe*, 24.6.1979

# Parliament – House of Commons

MPs say they can't afford to live on their salaries, but neither can anyone else.

*Maureen Colquhoun*, 27.7.1975

The opportunity to sleep nine hours a night and really relax has been extremely good for me. I ask you to disabuse yourself of any idea that prison is harmful.

*John Stonehouse*, 3.8.1975

I had better recall, before someone else does, that I said on one occasion that all was fair in love, war and parliamentary procedure.

*Michael Foot*, 7.9.1975

We don't refer to each other's families here. Perhaps it's just as well.

*George Thomas, Speaker*, 9.5.1976

It is impossible to assume that an MP would never be bribed.

*Lord Salmon*, 24.10.1976

# Parliament – House of Lords

The House of Lords is a perfect eventide home.

*Baroness Stocks*, 4.10.1970

I could never be shouted down in the other place and I'm not going to be shouted down here.

*Lord George-Brown*, 22.11.1970

The only reform I want is to abolish the House of Lords.

*Lord Wigg*, 23.6.1974

We are nothing much to look at and most of us are not very young any more. We are not very exciting to listen to and many of us are not great orators but we do have dignity.

*Lord Denham*, 23.3.1975

A House which is incapable of exercising any sort of influence is a House that might just as well be abolished.

*Lord Goodman*, 16.11.1975

I went to the Lords because I had nowhere else to go.

*Lord Shinwell*, 9.10.1977

## Patriotism

The single most important impediment to global institutions is the concept of 'my country, right or wrong'.

*U Thant*, 2.1.1972

I wish all Poles could have the unity, freedom and the sovereignty that Poland deserves.

*Pope John Paul II*, 10.6.1979

## Pious Hopes

I promise to continue the work of my father with the same energy and the same intransigence for the fortune and long survival of our immortal country.

*Jean-Claude Duvalier, President-elect of Haiti*, 25.4.1971

Let no one expect to make his fortune—or his reputation— by selling America short.

*Richard Nixon*, 22.8.1971

Let others spend their time dealing with murky, small, unimportant things. We have spent our time and will spend our time building a better world.

*Richard Nixon*, 5.8.1973

For God's sake don't try to apply logic to Rhodesia.

*Roy Welensky*, 17.11.1974

In view of the success of my economic revolution in
Uganda, I offer myself to be appointed Head of the
Commonwealth.

*Idi Amin*, 13.4.1975

It is always nice to discuss principles when you can find
the time to do so.

*Edward Short*, 26.10.1975

My main concern is that my people should remain a nation
of farmers and break loose from the itch of town life.

*President Felix Houphouet-Boigny of the Ivory Coast*,
22.1.1978

The true spirit of cricket requires the bowler to aim at or
near the stumps, rather than the batsman's head.

*Professor Aubrey Jenkins*, 18.6.1978

The lorry strike would end immediately if the haulage
bosses were told to pay the money that is being claimed.

*Dennis Skinner, MP*, 14.1.1979

# Plus ça change . . .

The twentieth century may not be a very good thing but
it's the only century we've got.

*Norman St John-Stevas*, 11.10.1970

We will be making sure that the bad language is removed
by the next performance.

*Management of the Leeds Playhouse, after complaints
about Chaucer's 'Pardoner's Tale'*, 18.7.1971

Politicians and journalists have a peculiar dependence on,
and contempt for, each other.

*Alastair Burnet*, 5.12.1971

41

One of the strange things of life in the modern world, you must remember, is that there are some people who like to be colonies of Great Britain.

*Alec Douglas-Home, on Gibraltar,* 5.3.1972

I am fully retired now, thank God. Who on earth would want to be in business with the working men of today?

*Sir Bernard Docker,* 18.3.1973

I doubt if five per cent of the *Tribune* group have ever read *Das Kapital,* or that more than one per cent of those who have, really understood what Marx was writing about.

*Lord Shinwell,* 5.10.1975

Don't forget that we have been killing each other here for years.

*Ian Smith,* 9.7.1978

There are always rats in the West End.

*Spokesman for Westminster City Council,* 11.2.1979

I used to say that politics was the second oldest profession, and I have come to know that it bears a gross similarity to the first.

*Ronald Reagan,* 13.5.1979

## Police and Crime

Those who participate in riots and affrays do so at their peril.

*Lord Justice Sachs,* 23.8.1970

Penalties against possession of a drug should not be more damaging to an individual than the use of the drug itself.

*Jimmy Carter,* 7.8.1977

We are prepared to shoot and kill in the interests of society, if necessary.

*John Alderson, Chief Constable, Devon and Cornwall,*
25.2.1979

The chances of being raped are nine in 10,000. People should not be unduly alarmed.

> *Gilbert Kelland, Assistant Commissioner (Crime), New Scotland Yard, 4.3.1979*

Being a thief is a terrific life, but the trouble is they do put you in the nick for it.

> *John McVicar, 11.3.1979*

I shall never eliminate corruption in the Metropolitan Police. All we can hope is to reduce it and keep it as low as possible.

> *Sir David McNee, Metropolitan Police Commissioner, 22.4.1979*

## Politics and Politicians

You don't lead people by following them, but by saying what they want to follow.

> *Enoch Powell, 6.12.1970*

It is a bizarre biological fact that the Conservative Party can be directed along a sensible left-wing path only by a leader with impeccable aristocratic connections.

> *Humphrey Berkeley, 21.2.1971*

I believe no one is indispensable to the party. Even the leader of the party could disappear and 24 hours later it would be forgotten.

> *Lord Shinwell, 20.2.1972*

Mr Heath is better placed than anyone in public life to say that opinion polls are unreliable.

> *John Grigg, historian and journalist, 5.3.1972*

I never refer to public opinion polls.

> *Edward Heath, 19.3.1972*

Let it be bluntly stated that until dictatorship has been formally inaugurated in this country, a letter from the Prime Minister, unless backed by law, has no more force than a letter from me.

> *Enoch Powell, 24.12.1972*

I don't think Prime Ministers go until they're pushed.

*Jo Grimond*, 23.12.1973

The current political situation is the most refreshingly
uncertain period in the whole of the Liberal Party's history.

*Jeremy Thorpe*, 14.7.1974

Wishes in politicians are very fickle things, my friends.

*Ian Paisley*, 14.11.1976

Historically, I shall be associated with failure, but
someone ought to make the point that I had a go.

*Lord George-Brown*, 17.11.1977

Few politicians are masochists.

*Sir Harold Wilson*, 1.1.1978

I don't want to be Prime Minister again. It's pretty
tough going.

*Indira Gandhi*, 26.1.1978

It is not the business of politicians to please everyone.

*Margaret Thatcher*, 29.1.1978

The Labour Party must be one of the worst employers
in the country.

*Leslie Huckfield, MP (Lab)*, 7.1.1979

You may have to fight a battle more than once to win it.

*Margaret Thatcher*, 14.1.1979

# Poverty

You really can't talk about us as a privileged class any
more. Many of us are living in the most dreadful, the
most appalling discomfort.

*The Duke of Grafton*, 6.10.1974

44

# The Press

Newspapers which carry out investigative journalism will never be popular—with politicians or the police or the Civil Service or the legal fraternity or company boards—but they still perform a useful function.

*Alastair Hetherington, Editor, The Guardian,* 2.12.1973

The incredible increase in the cost of newsprint has set a time bomb ticking under national newspapers. The time bomb being that we employ too many people and pay them too much money. At the maximum, we have two years in which to put our house in order.

*Jocelyn Stevens,* 5.5.1974

The Government has been faced with an orchestrated campaign of pressures by the newspapers. They even had the gargantuan economic intellect of Bernard Levin squeaking away in the undergrowth like a demented vole.

*Denis Healey,* 13.6.1976

It would be a matter of great sadness if the character of *The Observer* was changed.

*Oliver McGregor, Chairman, Royal Commission on the Press,* 24.10.1976

Editors are entitled to be partisan.

*The Press Council,* 7.1.1979

Our position on *The Times* is like that of a man at the end of a windswept pier in some cold and out-of-season resort.

*William Rees-Mogg, Editor, The Times,* 4.3.1979

# 'and the Press said . . .'

In very truth the *Daily Express* is the voice of Britain.

*Daily Express headline,* 27.6.1971

Books of the day this week will appear tomorrow.

*The Guardian,* 7.1.1973

If people say what they wish, the heavens will not fall.

*People's Daily, Peking,* 7.1.1979

# Race

The uniform of colour, because it is involuntary and
irremovable, becomes an irresistible force for dominating
and disciplining those who wear it.

*Enoch Powell*, 23.1.1977

I have never seen a white man and would be most alarmed
if I turned white myself.

*A J P Taylor*, 26.2.1978

Life in the South is much better now, for both blacks and
whites. Martin always said it would be a fine place to live
when the prejudice was gone.

*Mrs Martin Luther King*, 9.4.1978

# Religion

Lord, we have cruelly established the economic stability
of many powerful nations upon the trading of arms to poor
nations lacking ploughs, schools and hospitals.

*Pope Paul VI, in prayer*, 4.1.1970

I have rededicated my life to teaching as many people as
possible for Christ before I go to heaven.

*Billy Graham*, 19.4.1970

Clergy who take part in religious broadcasts often sound
like Arthur Askey on the loose. A canon reading the lesson
often sounds like an excerpt from 'All Gas and Gaiters'.

*George Reindorp, Bishop of Guildford*, 12.7.1970

Sometimes I have the devil of a job convincing ghosts they
are actually dead.

*Canon John Pearce-Higgins, on exorcising haunted
houses*, 9.12.1973

I'm suspicious of any religion that doesn't involve the use
of the mind.

*Michael Ramsey, Archbishop of Canterbury*, 9.6.1974

So far as a Catholic is concerned, the only thing to do
with a Protestant or an Anglican is to try to convert them.

*Archbishop Marcel Lefebvre*, 5.9.1976

More people go to worship God on a Sunday than attend
a football match on a Saturday.

*Very Rev Dr David Steel, former Moderator of the Church
of Scotland*, 12.2.1978

I cannot be angry at God, in whom I do not believe.

*Simone de Beauvoir*, 7.1.1979

The idea of Christ as a political figure, a revolutionary,
as the subversive man from Nazareth, does not tally with
the Church's catachesis.

*Pope John Paul II*, 4.2.1979

The Pope has made St Stanislaw into a model for the
enemies of governments.

*Polish Government spokesman*, 4.3.1979

We have so many forms to fill in and the excessive time
spent on paper-work means there is less time for prayer.

*Abbot Leo Smith of Buckfast Abbey*, 22.4.1979

# Royalty

There are always people around waiting for me to put my
foot in it, just like my father.

*Princess Anne*, 26.4.1970

Money for the Royal Family is an eternal dispute about
which one monarch lost his head.

*Richard Crossman*, 6.6.1971

I am not anti-socialist, but I regret to say that it was
nationalism and socialism which produced Nazis and
Fascists.

*The Duke of Edinburgh*, 19.8.1973

He kept telling me he was a confirmed batchelor and I
thought at least one knows where one stands.

*Princess Anne, on Captain Mark Phillips*, 18.11.1973

When Prince Andrew comes he always comes to the galley
and waves at us and shouts 'Hallo slaves'—only as a joke
of course. The Royal Family treat you like a person.

*Bill Carbery, Royal Train Steward*, 22.8.1976

Some people obviously do think that you can have a
totally egalitarian system. But no one has achieved it
above the level of a tribal society.

*The Duke of Edinburgh*, 23.1.1977

The monarchy is a labour-intensive industry.

*Harold Wilson*, 13.2.1977

When I appear in public people expect me to neigh, grind
my teeth, paw the ground and swish my tail.

*Princess Anne*, 22.3.1977

I cannot forget that I was crowned Queen of the United
Kingdom of Great Britain and Northern Ireland.

*The Queen*, 8.5.1977

Much of British management does not seem to understand
the human factor.

*The Prince of Wales*, 25.2.1979

Switch that bloody thing off you silly f——.

*The Duke of Edinburgh*, 4.3.1979

Things change so terribly fast these days. Look at the
Shah of Iran, poor man.

*Queen Elizabeth the Queen Mother*, 18.3.1979

## Shadows before

We now have a Rhodesian Constitution and if anybody
thinks it can be improved, I would like to know where.

*Ian Smith*, 18.4.1971

48

The industrial nations will have to realise that their era
of terrific progress and even more terrific wealth based on
cheap oil is finished.

*The Shah of Iran*, 30.12.1973

Perhaps this country needs an Iron Lady.

*Margaret Thatcher*, 28.3.1976

I hope to be Prime Minister one day and I do not want
there to be one street in Britain I cannot go down.

*Margaret Thatcher*, 1.5.1977

All Ugandans who believe in God should pray night and
day.

*Idi Amin*, 4.3.1979

# Signs of the Times

Funny really. When you look at the things that go on
these days my life story reads like Noddy.

*Diana Dors*, 15.3.1970

Most of us have stopped using silver every day.

*Margaret Thatcher*, 2.8.1970

The concept of marriage as a meal ticket and a licence to
copulate, prefixed by a brief spell of romance, is on its
way out.

*James Hemming, psychologist*, 6.12.1970

Mr Heath promised a land of milk and honey—and Mrs
Thatcher stopped the flow of milk.

*John Selway, Labour Party agent*, 10.10.1971

In the old days you knew a bomb hoax was a hoax. The
trouble is now that you have to take them so damn
seriously.

*House of Commons official*, 7.11.1971

As so few nowadays understand Greek, the Toxophily
Society will henceforth be entitled the Archery Society.

*Eton College Chronicle*, 24.6.1973

I have 14 other grandchildren and if I pay one penny now,
then I'll have 14 kidnapped grandchildren.

*Paul Getty, 29.7.1973*

We have just as many people shopping but one or two of
them are now only buying 30 Christmas puddings—in
the past they would have bought 30 hampers.

*Fortnum & Mason spokesman, 28.12.1975*

Why should a married woman want a mortgage in her own
name? We'll have husbands doing the housework next.

*Eric Nash, branch manager of the Magnet and Planet
Building Society, 4.1.1976*

I accepted a peerage through a combination of the
coincidence of circumstances leading to an aberration.

*Lord Briginshaw, 31.10.1976*

The old boy network works better in Japan than in the
United Kingdom.

*Tadao Kato, Japanese Ambassador in London, 29.10.1978*

The novel of recent years has become so candid that there
are now not many books which are unacceptable to adult
readers.

*Stanley Dibnah, public librarian, Huddersfield, 5.11.1978*

I question whether God himself would wish me to hide
behind the principles of non-violence while innocent
persons were being slaughtered.

*Abel Muzorewa, 5.11.1978*

Even I, I the Pope, to cross the streets of Rome to visit
a parish, have to be guarded and defended by so many
policemen. My God! All this is inconceivable.

*Pope John Paul II, 15.4.1979*

My older fans were disappointed when I started saying
four-letter words on stage, but they don't come to the
theatre very much any more and I've made an entirely
new public.

*Sir John Gielgud, 22.4.1979*

The moment for our industry has come again.

*Sir Peter Parker, Chairman, British Rail, 1.7.1979*

# South Africa

Regardless of how much South Africa may need expertise and skills, I will not allow in any person who admits to being an atheist. Tolerance and mutual respect are basic needs if people of different societies are to live in harmony.

*Piet Koornhof, South African Minister of Immigration,*
*10.9.1972*

South Africa has always been known as a country where we have proper and clean administration.

*P W Botha, South African Prime Minister, 25.3.1979*

When it came to the survival of South Africa, morality flew out of the window.

*Eschel Rhoodie, former South African Head of Information,*
*1.4.1979*

# Soviet Union

The Soviet Union is and has always been in favour of serious and honest negotiations among equal partners.

*Pravda, 7.2.1971*

Writers are much more esteemed here: they play a much larger part in society than they do in the West. The price of . . . er . . . the advantage of not being free is that people do listen to you.

*Lord Snow, interviewed on Radio Moscow, 15.8.1971*

There is no anti-semitism in Russia. In fact, many of my best friends are Jews.

*Alexei Kosygin, 24.10.1971*

Our relations with the Soviet Union are good: it does not mean we accept anything to do with their system; we abominate it.

*Harold Wilson, 14.3.1976*

I should like to reaffirm most definitely that the Soviet Union does not threaten anyone and is not going to attack anyone.

*Leonid Brezhnev, 2.1.1977*

The first characteristic of the Soviet Union is that it
always adopts the attitude of bullying the soft and fearing
the strong.

*Vice-Premier Den Xiaoping of China*, 4.2.1979

I have been a Kremlinologist for 42 years and I still cannot
guess what the Russians will do next.

*Sir Fitzroy Maclean*, 25.3.1979

# Sport

Boxing is not a sport, it is a criminal activity.

*Professor Ernst Jokl of Kentucky*, 13.9.1970

A sporting system is the by-product of society and its
political system, and it is just boyhood dreaming to suppose
you can ever take politics out of sport.

*Peter Hain*, 2.5.1971

Women athletes, except for very rare cases, are real women.

*Dr Christine Pickard*, 26.3.1972

It will probably be the great sports event in history.
Bigger than the Frazier–Ali fight. It is really the free world
against the lying, cheating, hypocritical Russians.

*Bobby Fischer, on the world chess championship*, 9.4.1972

I hit him in the chest because that slows the heart; I
went for the stomach to take his wind and I hit him in the
kidney area because that makes the kidneys swell.

*Ken Norton, explaining the tactics by which he defeated*
*Muhammad Ali*, 13.5.1973

We are living in a society which increasingly demands
success and no longer has time for the good loser.

*Tony Waddington, Manager, Stoke City Football Club*,
2.12.1973

I'd like to see new laws passed to fine soccer hooligans
anything from £50 to £100. I'd have no hesitation either
in putting these thugs in prison.

*Don Revie*, 25.8.1974

The most intelligent bit of spectator violence I ever heard of happened in Brazil. An enraged spectator drew his gun and shot the ball.

> *Professor John Cohen, Manchester University,* 1.9.1974

It will be open house—caviar, vodka, no problems about visas.

> *Mayor Vladimir Bromislov of Moscow, on*
> *the 1980 Olympics,* 27.10.1974

I have no interest in sailing round the world. Not that there is any lack of requests for me to do so.

> *Edward Heath,* 19.6.1977

As we ride, the air is blue with all sorts of language.

> *Joanna Morgan, first woman to ride in the Derby,*
> 15.4.1979

# Taxes

I'm tired of our taxing the poor people in our rich country and sending the money to rich people in poor countries.

> *Jimmy Carter,* 29.8.1976

# Terrorism

The men of violence are not going to bomb their way to the conference table. Nor must they be allowed to bomb Northern Ireland into the abyss.

> *Harold Wilson,* 21.4.1974

I find it very difficult to see the argument that terrorism would be uniquely responsive to a capital deterrent.

> *Roy Jenkins,* 21.7.1974

The romantic concept of the terrorist is an obstacle to his suppression.

> *Conor Cruise O'Brien,* 22.2.1976

Baader had the perfidy to shoot himself in the back of his head to try to make us look like murderers.

*Werner Maihofer, West German Interior Minister,*
*23.10.1977*

Terrorism by the leadership won't achieve the liberty of the Palestinian and his land. A bomb here and a bomb there won't help.

*Anwar Sadat, 8.4.1979*

I always find it unrealistic for a politician to rush in and condemn terrorism.

*Enoch Powell, 22.4.1979*

# Theatres and Players

The theatre should be necessary—like a bank or grocer's shop. It should provide something that people can't get anywhere else.

*Peter Brook, 30.8.1970*

As one gets older, one's standards get higher and you get less satisfied with your own achievements.

*John Neville, 6.9.1970*

We need to pray for all those concerned with the theatre that worthy standards may be maintained.

*Michael Ramsey, Archbishop of Canterbury, 20.9.1970*

I'd say award-winning plays are written only for the critics.

*Lew Grade, 18.10.1970*

If one wants to see people naked one doesn't go to the theatre, one goes to a Turkish bath.

*Noel Coward, 3.1.1971*

These days a star is anyone who can hold a microphone. A super-star is someone who has shaken hands with Lew Grade, and a super-super-star is someone who has refused to shake hands with Lew Grade.

*Harry Secombe, 19.3.1972*

54

I never deliberately set out to shock, but when people don't walk out of my plays I think there is something wrong.

*John Osborne*, 19.1.1975

I agree with the Bogart theory that all an actor owes the public is a good performance.

*Lauren Bacall*, 14.1.1979

Acting isn't really a very high-class way to make a living, is it?

*Katharine Hepburn*, 21.1.1979

If you play sexiness deliberately, the audience senses the phoniness.

*Sophia Loren*, 28.1.1979

I get quite annoyed, you know, when I am referred to as the founder of a dynasty.

*Sir Michael Redgrave*, 11.3.1979

Acting great parts devours you.

*Lord Olivier*, 1.4.1979

## Trade Unions

My lads come first. To hell with the critics.

*Clive Jenkins*, 22.3.1970

To be an official of a union representing lower paid workers is no career for a self-respecting man.

*Clive Jenkins*, 2.5.1971

The unions now have such overwhelming strength in relation to the employers that we are in a runaway situation. It is really surprising that they restrain themselves as much as they do.

*Lord Beeching*, 23.4.1972

No one should think that if our mates are in trouble in the mining industry the TUC will stand by with its arms folded.

*Len Murray*, 3.2.1974

I have only got one social contract which I honour and that is with the members of my union.

*Arthur Scargill*, 3.11.1974

There is a minority of trade unionists who believe that to break the social contract is a kind of virility symbol.

*Eric Varley*, 6.4.1975

Trade unionism is killing socialism in Britain, and it is time socialists did something about it.

*Paul Johnson*, 18.5.1975

Grunwick is a Dunkirk for the trade union movement.

*Jack Dromey, Secretary, Brent Trades Council*, 4.9.1977

If unions hold the whip hand, upon whose back does the lash fall?

*Margaret Thatcher*, 25.9.1977

Only a fool wants a confrontation and only a fool wants a strike.

*Arthur Scargill*, 6.11.1977

There isn't a man here would stand by to see someone burn to death. We all have consciences, but it doesn't buy bread.

*Leading Fireman Nick Deniet of Euston Fire Station*, 13.11.1977

Workers' control means the castration of the trade union movement.

*Arthur Scargill*, 23.4.1978

The rapacious prosecution of self-interest has nothing to do with trade unionism.

*Tom Jackson, Chairman, TUC*, 19.11.1978

I bought a second-hand Moskvich car just to scare the bosses.

*Jim Reilly, General Secretary, Scottish Union of Powerloom Overlookers*, 28.1.1979

Fathers ought to form a union and win the right to go home early if their children are sick.

*Dr Benjamin Spock*, 18.3.1979

# Travel

You'd think, with all these tourists about, they would build an elevator.

*American lady climbing up to the Parthenon*, 30.4.1972

No other form of transport in the rest of my life has ever come up to the bliss of my pram.

*Osbert Lancaster*, 25.1.1976

I remember an American said there is more upset to the ozone layer by cows breaking wind in fields than by a whole fleet of supersonic transports flying simultaneously.

*Archibald Russell, designer of Concorde*, 15.2.1976

# United States of America

I would rather be a one-term President than be a two-term President at the cost of seeing America become a second-rate power and see this nation accept the first defeat in its proud 190-year history.

*Richard Nixon*, 3.5.1970

I am fed up with a system which busts the pot-smoker and lets the big dope racketeers go free. I am sick of old men dreaming up wars for young men to die in.

*George McGovern*, 9.4.1972

The distinctive difference between a free man and a slave is the right to possess arms.

*Superintendent Colin Greenwood of Wakefield, Virginia*,
8.4.1973

I don't believe there's anything in the Constitution that says the powers of the Presidency be separated from the truth.

*Senator Sam Ervin of the Watergate Committee*,
15.7.1973

I don't give a damn about protocol. I'm a swinger. Bring out the beautiful spies.

*Henry Kissinger, on seating at official dinners*, 9.12.1973

I'm not running on the sainthood ticket. I'm a Democrat.

*Hubert Humphrey*, 8.2.1976

# Vengeance

We'll hang people. A few. We've still got a lot of chaps doing bad things.

*General Zia ul-Haq, military ruler of Pakistan, 30.4.1978*

We can say without any hesitation, beyond the shadow of a doubt, that Sadat has signed his own demise.

*President Hafez Assad of Syria, 1.4.1979*

If Kennedy runs, I'll whip his ass.

*Jimmy Carter, 17.6.1979*


# War and Peace

I seriously doubt if we will have another war. This [Vietnam] is probably the last.

*Richard Nixon, 14.3.1971*

If I have committed a crime it was because I valued my troops' lives more than enemy troops.

*Lieutenant William Calley, 4.4.1971*

If we have a guided weapon, what we want it to do is to hit the target. There is no need for it to play 'God Save The Queen' when it has done so.

*J P W Mallelieu, MP, 16.4.1972*

The most important thing in war preparation, in my opinion, is that we educate our people in the spirit of hating the enemy. Without educating our people in this spirit we cannot defeat the United States, which is superior in technology.

*Premier Kim Il Sung of North Korea, 4.6.1972*

It is not easy to achieve through negotiations what has not been achieved on the battlefield.

*Henry Kissinger, 28.1.1973*

When you are at war you don't call in the Salvation Army.

*Joshua Nkomo, 26.6.1977*

If you want to make peace, you don't talk to your friends.
You talk to your enemies.

*Moshe Dayan*, 16.10.1977

The central act of warfare, battle, is so unpleasant, so
degrading, so terrifying, that the majority of men will do
almost anything to avoid it if they can.

*John Keegan, Senior Lecturer in War Studies, Sandhurst,*
26.3.1978

It is salutory to remember that the Hiroshima explosion of
1945 is widely known in Japan as 'the Christian bomb'.

*Very Rev Lord MacLeod of Fuinary*, 30.7.1978

# Women

For every woman trying to free women there are probably
two trying to restrict someone else's freedom.

*Brigid Brophy*, 25.10.1970

All Berkshire women are very silly. I don't know why
women in Berkshire are more silly than anywhere else.

*Judge Claude Duveen, in Reading County Court*, 9.7.1972

I have noticed signs of ageing in the last two years and
even feel a little frightened when a new wrinkle appears.

*Brigitte Bardot*, 22.4.1973

Women in Communist and Western countries do men's
work. They wear men's haircuts. Islamic law gives women
the right to express themselves, but not in chemistry,
cement and tar. No, no, no. Women have only human
rights.

*Colonel Muammar al-Qadhafi of Libya*, 8.7.1973

Today women give up too easily. I think they should play
harder to get.

*The Duchess of Windsor*, 28.4.1974

I've a woman's ability to stick to a job and get on with it
when everyone else walks off and leaves it.

*Margaret Thatcher*, 16.2.1975

Women on the whole tend to be nicer and more important,
nearer to God than men. That they are gentler no one
will deny.

*Lord Arran*, 20.7.1975

I'll wager you that in 10 years it will be fashionable again
to be a virgin.

*Barbara Cartland*, 20.6.1976

I like my ladies to be feminine. I don't like a lady
policeman—that is a contradiction in terms.

*David McNee, Metropolitan Police Commissioner*,
18.6.1978

Being a sex symbol was rather like being a convict.

*Racquel Welch*, 25.2.1979

# Ah, Youth

A continued attack on the young—not in their attitudes
so much as their motives—can serve little purpose other
than to cement those attitudes to a solidity impossible to
penetrate with reason.

*Walter Hickel, US Interior Secretary*, 10.5.1970

Today's youth will not tolerate the privations of my
generation.

*Hugh Scanlon*, 7.5.1978

# Index

Keegan, John, 59
Kelland, Gilbert, 43
Kenyatta, Jomo, 21
Khomeini, Ayatollah, 20
King, Mrs Martin Luther, 46
Kingsway Tunnel, Liverpool, 37
Kissinger, Henry, 21, 57, 58
Koestler, Arthur, 20
Koornhof, Piet, 51
Korchnoi, Anatov, 32
Kosygin, Alexei, 51

Lancaster, Osbert, 57
Leatherland, Lord, 16
Leeds Playhouse, 41
Lefebvre, Marcel, 47
Lennon, John, 36
Lever, Harold, 35
Lindop, Tom, 15
*Liverpool Free Press*, 34
Longford, Lord, 30, 34
Loren, Sophia, 55
Lovell, Sir Bernard, 11, 21
Lynch, Jack, 25

McGovern, George, 5, 57
McGregor, Oliver, 45
McKinney, Joyce, 31
Maclean, Sir Fitzroy, 52
MacLeod of Fuinary, Lord, 59
Macmillan, Harold, 8, 21, 35
McNee, David, 43, 60
MacStiofain, Sean, 25
McVicar, John, 43
Maihofer, Werner, 54
Makarios, Archbishop, 37
Mallelieu, J P W, 58
Manson, Charles, 37
Mao Tse Tung, 37
Marsh, Richard, 10
Marx, Groucho, 27
Matthews, George, 11
Maudling, Reginald, 17
Mauriac, François, 32
Millett, Kate, 31
Milne, Christopher Robin, 39
Montefiore, Hugh, 19
Morgan, Joanna, 53
Morley, Robert, 8

Morris, Max, 13, 14
Morris, Robert, 6
Mortimer, John, 30
Muggeridge, Malcolm, 21
Murley, Reginald, 30
Murray, Len, 18, 23, 55
Muzorewa, Abel, 11, 50

Nabarro, Gerald, 26
Nagy, Richard, 10
Nash, Eric, 50
Nasser, Gamal Abdel, 36
Nene College computer, 19
Neville, John, 54
Neville, Richard, 7
*New Soviet Encyclopaedia*, 8
Nixon, Richard, 33, 34, 38, 40, 57, 58
Nkomo, Joshua, 58
Norton, Ken, 52

O'Brien, Conor Cruise, 53
O'Brien, Edna, 27
Olivier, Lord, 55
Onassis, Aristotle, 20
Osborne, John, 29, 55
Owen, David, 18

Paisley, Ian, 24, 44
Park, Mr Justice, 28
Parker, Sir Peter, 50
Paton, William, 29
Paul VI, Pope, 17, 46
Payne, Mr Justice, 31
Pearce-Higgins, John, 46
Peart, Fred, 17
Pentagon Papers, 9
*People's Daily*, Peking, 45
Perelman, S J, 9
Peterson, Peter, 14
Pickard, Christine, 52
Polanski, Roman, 6
Pompidou, Georges, 9, 11, 32
Porter, Sir George, 14
Powell, Enoch, 15, 43, 46, 54
*Pravda*, 51
Prentice, Reg, 22
Press Council, 45
Pyke, Magnus, 17

Qadhafi, Muammar al-, 59